dip in and go.
by Alison Hedger

- **2 Lotty's Shadow Dance** – Dancing with a partner
- **4 Always Ask Me** – Song using major and minor keys
- **8 The Irish Jig** – Lively dance with an irregular rhythmic pattern
- **10 I Went To The Beach** – An accumulating song
- **15 Teddy's Exercise Poem** – A fun action poem
- **16 Loch Scridan** – Three-part round with flute/recorder counter-melody
- **19 Water Is Heavy And Noisy!** – Poem and percussion
- **20 Little Lamb** – Song with words by William Blake (Optional second part)
- **24 Three Brothers** – Discovering pitch
- **27 Fred** – Hilarious action poem
- **28 The Choo-Choo Train** Action song

CHESTER MUSIC
part of The Music Sales Group
London / New York / Paris / Sydney / Copenhagen / Berlin / Madrid / Tokyo

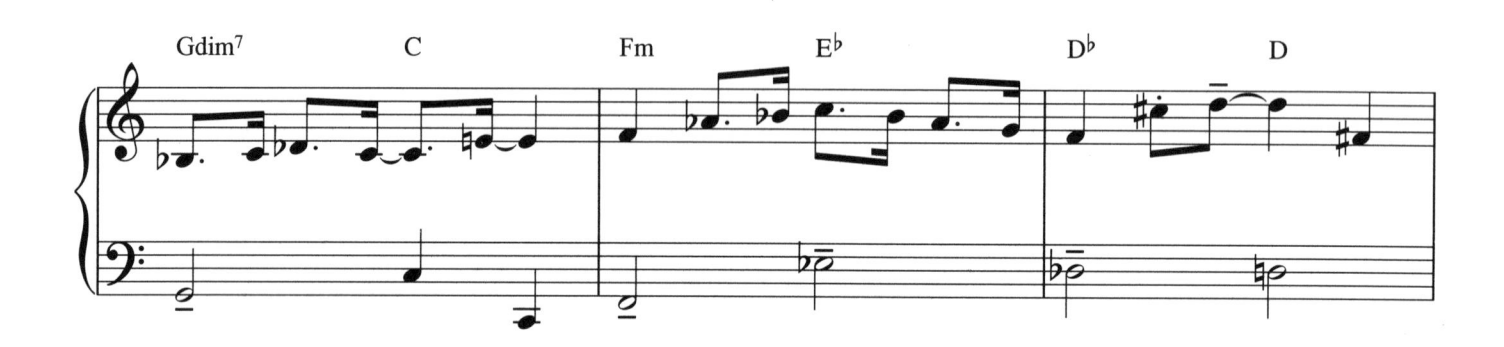

LOTTY'S SHADOW DANCE

Dancing with a partner one behind the other

How to do LOTTY'S SHADOW DANCE

Preliminary Work

*Unlike a lot of other imitation activities, in LOTTY'S SHADOW DANCE the children stand one **behind** the other, not face to face.*

Work out with the children how a shadow makes a direct copy (which may be distorted in size depending on the light source). Have fun yourself making movements and ask the class to say if a following child is imitating your actions.

Dancing in Pairs

Play the music and organise the children into pairs, one behind the other. Let the leading children experiment with suitable movements, large and small, high and low, twisted and straight, wide and narrow, stiff and floppy etc. which interpret the music. Partners change places and continue with the new leaders. Look out for some interesting physical actions which reflect the mood of the music.

ALWAYS ASK ME

Song using major and minor keys and a visual aid

The sentiments in the lyrics are echoed in the music. The MINOR KEY reflects the unhappy selfishness, the MAJOR KEY reflects the happy state. Whilst defining minor music as "sad" and major music as "happy" is too much of a generalisation, it does make an excellent starting point with children.

Follow the mood of the words ♩ = 122

MINOR KEY

1. "Don't ask me," said the self-ish boy,— "I have-n't time to help you."—
2. "Don't ask me," said the self-ish girl,— "I have-n't time to help you."—

So this boy was al-ways a-lone— and grew un-hap-py and sad.—
So this girl was al-ways a-lone— and grew un-hap-py and sad.—

MAJOR KEY

"Always ask me," said the generous boy, "it won't take long for me to help." So this boy was never alone, he was happy and too busy to be sad.

"Always ask me," said the generous girl, "it won't take long for me to help." So this girl was never alone, she was happy and too busy to be sad.

(D.C.)

Lyrics for ALWAYS ASK ME

1. "Don't ask me," said the selfish boy,
   "I haven't time to help you."
   So this boy was always alone
   And grew unhappy and sad.
   "Always ask me," said the generous boy,
   "It won't take long for me to help."
   So this boy was never alone,
   He was happy and too busy to be sad.

2. "Don't ask me," said the selfish girl,
   "I haven't time to help you."
   So this girl was always alone
   And grew unhappy and sad.
   "Always ask me," said the generous girl,
   "It won't take long for me to help."
   So this girl was never alone,
   She was happy and too busy to be sad.

Activity

Draw two line pictures like those on the opposite page.

Increase the size as necessary and use as cut-outs. You will need two boys and two girls. Read the lyrics and draw on the relevant downcast mouth. Children may like to add eyes to complete the faces.

Ask the children which boy or girl would they like to be? This visual aid really makes an impression and pinpoints the children's attention to the difference in sound between the major and minor keys when they are learning the song.

7

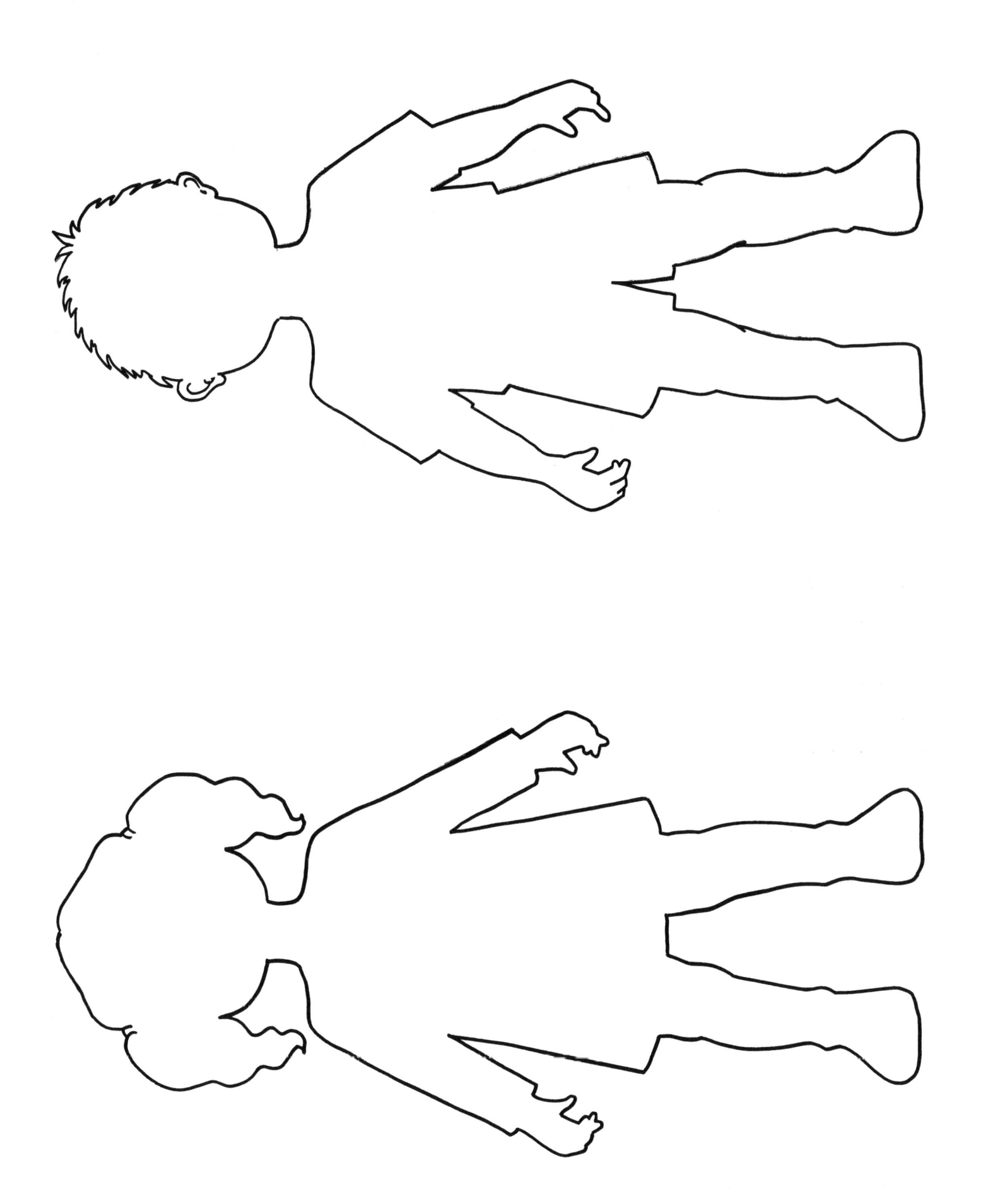

THE IRISH JIG

Lively dance with an irregular rhythmic pattern

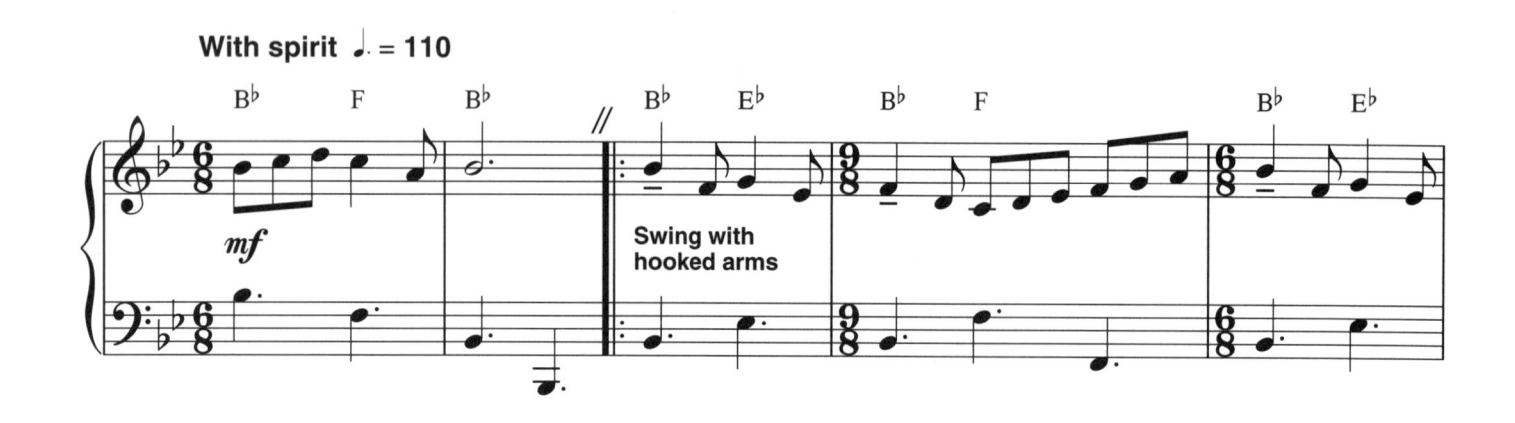

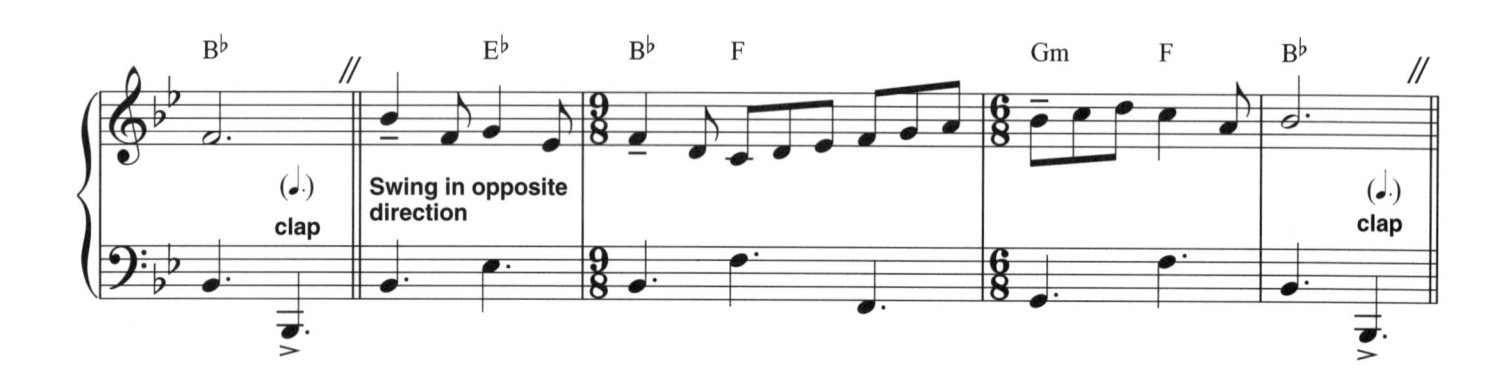

REPEAT as required

Activities for THE IRISH JIG

The recurring rhythmic counting pattern is as follows:

one-two | one-two-three | one-two | one-two

The children need to be familiar with counting along to the music before starting to dance. You will be happily surprised at how quickly children grasp an irregular pattern, especially one that has a constant repeat.

DANCE INSTRUCTIONS

Based on the above rhythmic counting pattern repeated four times.

1. Children are in pairs. They swing around with hooked arms for one counting pattern, finishing with a hearty clap. (The CD recording will make the hand claps obvious.)

2. Children reverse swing with their other arms hooked for the next counting pattern, finishing with another hand clap.

3. Standing opposite their partner, each child keeps time with the beats:
slap knees, clap
slap knees, clap, clap hands with partner
slap knees, clap
slap knees three times to coincide with the music

4. Repeat instruction 3 above.

BEGIN DANCE OVER AGAIN

(Upper Primary children will have fun being inventive and creating their own dances to the recurring rhythmic pattern.)

FURTHER LISTENING ACTIVITIES

Here is another example of an irregular rhythm, created by alternating groups of 3 and 2 beats:

Ask children to create their own irregular rhythmic patterns using classroom percussion instruments.

For Golden Apple examples of music grouped in fives, (which is simply a combination of 2 and 3 beats), listen to:

WATER in Harvest Time GA11086
THE SILLY MILLIPEDE in Minibeast Madness GA11090
ONLY THE START in Bathsheba! GA11374

Tchaikovsky's 6th Symphony, The "Pathetique", has its second movement in 5/4 time. This was thought loathsome at its first performance in 1893!

I WENT TO THE BEACH
A accumulating song

Pictures and articles can be held up at the appropriate time!

1. Slimy seaweed
2. Old driftwood
3. Shiny shells
4. Broken oars
5. Mooring rope
6. Blue flip-flops
7. Ten pound note

With enthusiasm ♩ = 120

1. I went to the beach and found some slim-y sea-weed. 2. I went to the beach and

D/F♯ D A7 D A Em9 A7 D A7
found some old drift-wood and slim-y sea-weed. 3. I
D Em7 A7 D/F♯ D A7 D A D A
went to the beach and found some shin-y shells, some old drift-wood and
Em9 A7 D A7 D Em7 A7 D/F♯ D A7
slim-y sea-weed. 4. I went to the beach and found some
D A D A D A Em9 A7
brok-en oars, some shin-y shells, some old drift-wood and slim-y sea-

-weed. 5. I went to the beach and found some moor-ing rope, some brok-en oars, some shin-y shells, some old drift-wood and slim-y sea-weed. 6. I went to the beach and found some blue flip-flops, some moor-ing rope, some brok-en oars, some shin-y shells, some old drift-wood and slim - y sea - weed. 7. I went to the beach and found a ten pound note, some blue flip - flops, some moor - ing rope, some brok - en oars, some shin - y shells, some old drift - wood and slim - y sea - weed.

Lyrics for I WENT TO THE BEACH

1. I went to the beach and found
   Some slimy seaweed.

2. I went to the beach and found
   Some old driftwood
   And slimy seaweed.

3. I went to the beach and found
   Some shiny shells,
   Some old driftwood
   And slimy seaweed.

4. I went to the beach and found
   Some broken oars,
   Some shiny shells,
   Some old driftwood
   And slimy seaweed.

5. I went to the beach and found
   Some mooring rope,
   Some broken oars,
   Some shiny shells,
   Some old driftwood
   And slimy seaweed.

6. I went to the beach and found
   Some blue flip-flops,
   Some mooring rope,
   Some broken oars,
   Some shiny shells,
   Some old driftwood
   And slimy seaweed.

7. I went to the beach and found
   A ten pound note,
   Some blue flip-flops,
   Some mooring rope,
   Some broken oars,
   Some shiny shells,
   Some old driftwood
   And slimy seaweed.

TEDDY'S EXERCISE POEM

To be done with actions at least 3 times: slowly, at medium speed and very fast.

Teddy is a clever bear
He exercises everywhere   (exercise ankles, wrists, neck etc)

Teddy's up and Teddy's down   (crouch down)
Teddy wears a fancy crown   (use hands to make a crown)

Teddy's down and Teddy's up   (stand up)
Teddy's drinking from his cup   (mime drinking)

Teddy's wide and Teddy's thin   (spread arms and legs)
Teddy's proud of being slim   (show off with hands on hips)

Teddy reaches very high   (stretch to full extent)
Teddy reaches to the sky

Teddy falls upon the floor   (sink to ground level)
Time to say this all once more!

LOCH SCRIDAN

Three-part round with flute/recorder counter-melody

Full of fun! ♩ = 114

PART ONE

As I rowed my boat up the Loch Scri - dan, I heard the shout of a Scot - tish man: "What - cha got there?" he yelled with a grin. So I tipped up my bag to show him ev - 'ry - thing.

PART TWO

Flan and ham and a juic - y peach, slip - pers and a kip - per and a bag of sweets; a flan - nel for my face and a pil - low for my head, a bot - tle of ketch - up 'cause I like my food red!

PART THREE

Keys and cheese and a pair of clean socks, pants and vest and sec-ur-it-y locks; bread and but-ter and a lit-tle camp bed, a pic-ture of my Moth-er, and my

to repeat: fav-our-ite Ted. As I

to finish: fav-our-ite Ted.

Flute/Recorder Counter-melody

Full of fun! ♩ = 114

mf

cresc.

(As I)

Lyrics for LOCH SCRIDAN

Written to mark the 40th anniversary of Hordle Walhampton School's Mull camp overlooking Loch Scridan.

1. As I rowed my boat up the Loch Scridan,
   I heard the shout of a Scottish man:
   "What-cha got there?" he yelled with a grin.
   So I tipped up my bag to show him everything.

2. Flan and ham and a juicy peach,
   Slippers and a kipper and a bag of sweets;
   A flannel for my face and a pillow for my head,
   A bottle of ketchup 'cause I like my food red!

3. Keys and cheese and a pair of clean socks,
   Pants and vest and security locks;
   Bread and butter and a little camp bed,
   A picture of my Mother, and my favourite Ted.

Loch Scridan on the Isle of Mull, Scotland, is also known as:
   Loch Scridain
   Loch Scedon
   Loch Screden
   Loch Seriden

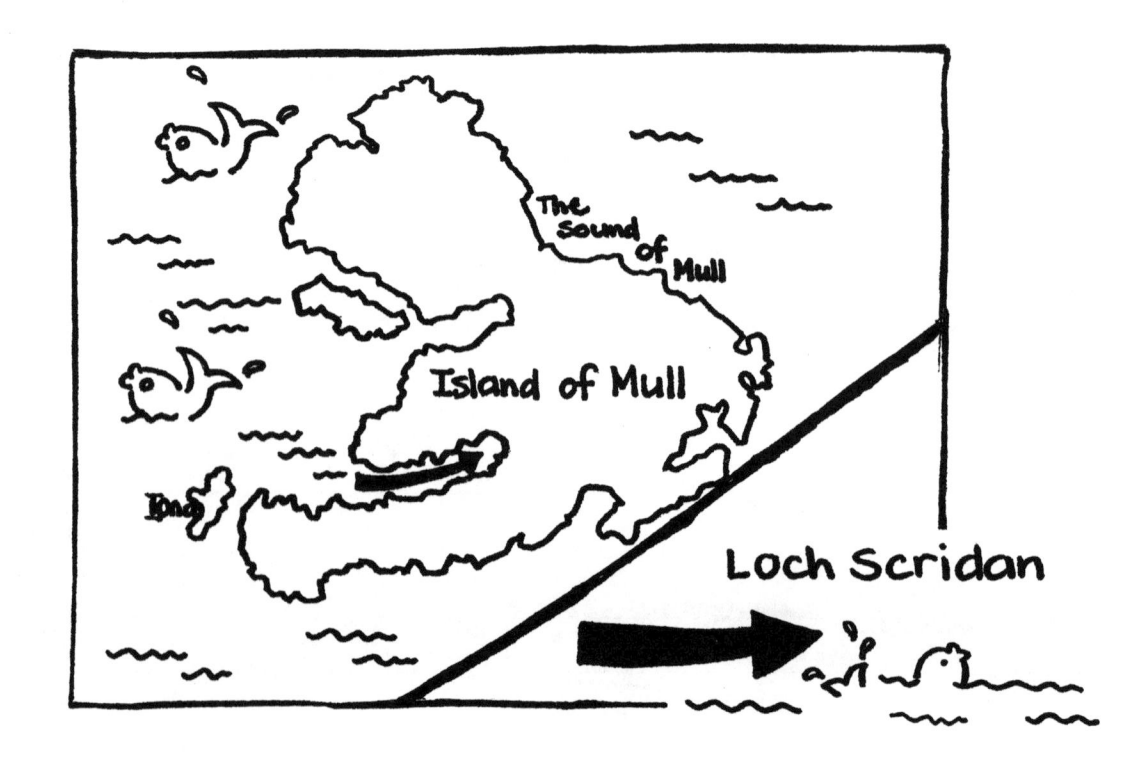

WATER IS HEAVY AND NOISY!
Poem and percussion

"Fill this bucket up with water;
Come and help me, little daughter."
But the bucket filled with water
Was too heavy for my daughter.
Heavy water,
Little daughter:
"Try to carry just a quarter."
But a quarter of the water
Still was heavy for my daughter!
So instead, I went and brought her
Just a tumbler of clear water.
This she drank, and said I'd taught her
Just how heavy weighed pure water.

The children sit in a circle around a selection of school percussion instruments.

- Discuss the weight difference between an empty bucket and one filled with water. Ask the children: Which instruments could illustrate *heavy* and which *light*?
- How could we make the sound of a dripping tap?
- How can we make a difference between the sound of a dripping tap and the sound of falling rain?
- Who has some ideas of how to represent a muddy, swirling river?
- What about rolling waves?
- Using music, how would you represent a clear, cool, sparkling brook?
- In small groups, each group decides which aspect of water they are going to illustrate with instruments – the rest of the class will see if they can guess the answer just by listening to the music.
- Has anyone thought of frozen water (sleet, frost, snow and ice)?
- What about a nice warm bath?
- Finish the session with storm music; start quietly with just a few drops of rain. Introduce the vocal sound of wind which gradually builds as more and more instruments join in. Don't forget a wobble board or sheets of paper for the lightning. This activity will be very noisy! Devise a cut off sound (whistle or gong) to stop the storm. With older children the storm can gradually cease, rather than be cut off in full flow. Make a balanced piece of music; encourage the children to decrease the volume by dropping out instruments and sound sources one by one, leaving the few "drops of rain" that began the storm. End in silence. Peace at last!

LITTLE LAMB

Song with optional second vocal part
Words by William Blake (1757–1827) from "Songs of Innocence"

Tenderly ♩ = 122

1. Lit - tle Lamb, who made thee?
Dost thou know who made thee? Gave thee life, and
2. Lit - tle Lamb, I'll tell thee,
Lit - tle Lamb, I'll tell thee: He is call - èd

20

bid thee feed, by the stream and o'er the mead;
by thy name, for He calls Him-self a Lamb.

Two parts

gave thee cloth-ing of de-light, soft-est cloth-ing,
He is meek and He is mild; He be-came a

wool-ly, bright; gave thee such a ten-der voice,
lit-tle child. I a child, and thou a lamb,

mak - ing all the vales re - joice? Lit - tle Lamb who made thee? Dost thou know who made thee?
we are call - èd by His name. Lit - tle Lamb, God bless thee. Lit - tle Lamb, God bless thee.

Lyrics for LITTLE LAMB

1. Little Lamb, who made thee?
   Dost thou know who made thee?
   Gave thee life, and bid thee feed
   By the stream and o'er the mead;
   Gave thee clothing of delight,
   Softest clothing, woolly, bright;
   Gave thee such a tender voice,
   Making all the vales rejoice?
   Little Lamb, who made thee?
   Dost thou know who made thee?

2. Little Lamb, I'll tell thee,
   Little Lamb, I'll tell thee:
   He is callèd* by thy name,
   For He calls himself a Lamb.
   He is meek and He is mild,
   He became a little child;
   I a child, and thou a lamb,
   We are callèd by His name.
   Little Lamb, God bless thee.
   Little Lamb, God bless thee.

   *Callèd = two syllables: "call-ed"

THREE BROTHERS
(Doh, Ray, Me)
A fun introduction to the concept of pitch

In a very jolly manner! ♩ = 120

Doh, Ray, Me are hap-py broth-ers, each one looks a lot like the oth-ers. We can hear an in-ter-est-ing thing when they op-en their mouths to sing.

Doh on-ly sings on the low-est note;___ Ray sings a lit-tle bit high-er;___ Me al-ways sings by him-self on the top.___ Doh, Ray, Me: they nev-er want to stop! Doh Ray, Me. Doh, Ray, Me.

Lyrics for THREE BROTHERS

Doh, Ray, Me are happy brothers,
Each one looks a lot like the others.
We can hear an interesting thing
When they open their mouths to sing.

Doh only sings on the lowest note;
Ray sings up a little higher;
Me always sings by himself on the top.
Doh, Ray, Me: they never want to stop!

Doh, Ray, Me.
Doh, Ray, Me.

Use hand signals for the three pitches: low (doh), medium (ray) and high (me).

DOH   RAY   ME

(CHIME BARS)

DOH   RAY   ME

FRED
A hilarious action poem for anytime

The opening and link to each verse is counting to eight. Different percussive sounds could be used on each number to represent the machinery in the bakery. Select sounds which are fun and which sound effective next to each other. Use a deep voice for the baker.

One, two, three, four, five, six, seven, eight.

1. Hi there! My name's Fred, I work in the bakery making bread.
   In came the baker and said "Hello. Fred, can you help me make some dough?"
   I said "Yes! I'll get it fixed, with my RIGHT HAND I can mix".

   One, two, three, four, five, six, seven, eight.
   (Right hand is mixing.)

2. Hi there! My name's Fred, I work in the bakery making bread.
   In came the baker and said "Hello. Fred can you help me make some dough?"
   I said "Yes! I'll get it fixed, with my LEFT HAND I can mix."

   One, two, three, four, five, six, seven, eight.
   (Left hand joins right hand in mixing.)

3. Hi there! My name's Fred, I work in the bakery making bread.
   In came the baker and said "Hello. Fred can you help me make some dough?"
   I said "Yes! I'll get it fixed, with my RIGHT FOOT I can mix."

   One, two, three, four, five, six, seven, eight.
   (Right foot joins hands in mixing.)

4. Hi there! My name's Fred, I work in the bakery making bread.
   In came the baker and said "Hello. Fred can you help me make some dough?"
   I said "Yes! I'll get it fixed, with my LEFT FOOT I can mix."

   One, two, three, four, five, six, seven, eight.
   (Left foot joins hands and right foot in the mixing.)

5. Hi there! My name's Fred, I work in the bakery making bread.
   In came the baker and said "Hello. Fred can you help me make some dough?"
   I said "Yes! I'll get it fixed, with my BIG HEAD I can mix."

   One, two, three, four, five, six, seven, eight.
   (Head joins hands and feet in mixing.)

6. Hi there! My name's Fred, I work in the bakery making bread.
   In came the baker and said "Hello. Fred can you help me make some dough?"
   I said "NO!"

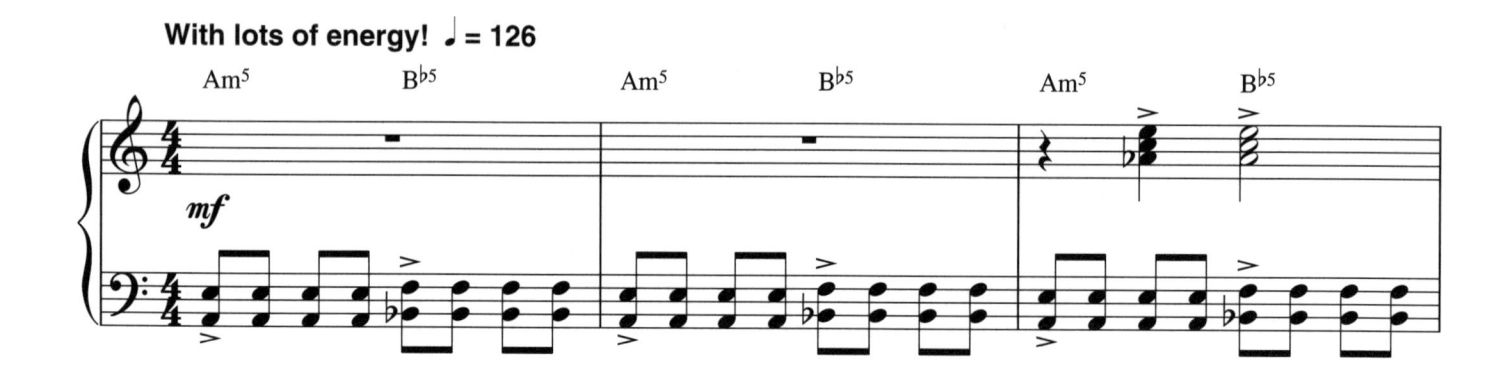

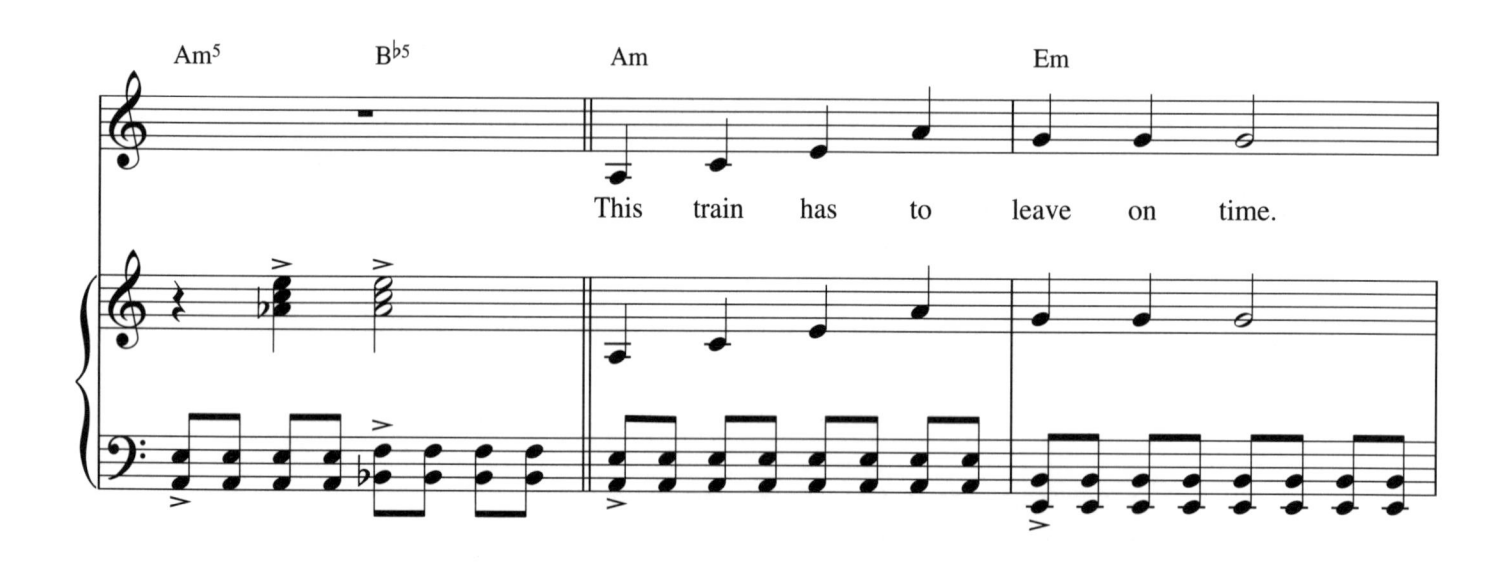

THE CHOO-CHOO TRAIN

With lots of energy! ♩ = 126

This train has to leave on time. Hold on tight, you'll be just fine! Running down the track is the train full of pas-sen-gers. Choo, choo, choo, choo, choo, choo, choo.

There's no charge, so hop on board. Don't for-get to shut the

doors. Oo - oo, Oo - oo,

Repeat as necessary   *rall.*

Oo - oo, Oo - oo. Whoosh!

dim. al fine

29

Lyrics for THE CHOO-CHOO TRAIN

**This train has to leave on time.
Hold on tight, you'll be just fine.**

**Running down the track is the train full of passengers.
Choo, choo, choo, choo, choo, choo, choo.
There's no charge, so hop on board.
Don't forget to shut the doors.**

Oo-oo, Oo-oo, Oo-oo, Oo-oo.
(To end) **Whoosh!**

The children make a single file train and let off steam with the train whistle. Great fun!

A controlled yet unusual way to get children from their classroom into the hall/gym. Alternatively the children could perform this activity around the playground, or inside the school building on a wet afternoon.

Older children can make a figure of eight around two chairs positioned at either end of a large clear area. With great precision they cross each other's path (no colliding), as if in a military display team.

Published by
Chester Music Limited
8/9 Frith Street, London W1D 3JB, England.

Exclusive Distributors:
Music Sales Limited
Distribution Centre, Newmarket Road, Bury St Edmunds, Suffolk IP33 3YB, England.
Music Sales Corporation
257 Park Avenue South, New York, NY10010, United States of America.
Music Sales Pty Limited
120 Rothschild Avenue, Rosebery, NSW 2018, Australia.

Order No. CH68299
ISBN 1-84449-484-5
This book © Copyright 2004 by Chester Music.

Unauthorised reproduction of any part of this publication by any means
including photocopying is an infringement of copyright.

Written by Alison Hedger.
Illustrations by Hilary Lack.
Music processed by Camden Music.
Cover designed by Fresh Lemon.
Printed in the United Kingdom by Caligraving Limited, Thetford, Norfolk.

CD recorded, mixed and mastered by Jonas Persson.
Music arranged by John Maul.
Vocals by Elly Barnes and Mike Winsor.

Your Guarantee of Quality
As publishers, we strive to produce every book to the highest commercial standards.
The music has been freshly engraved and the book has been carefully designed to
minimise awkward page turns and to make playing from it a real pleasure.
Particular care has been given to specifying acid-free, neutral-sized paper made from
pulps which have not been elemental chlorine bleached. This pulp is from farmed
sustainable forests and was produced with special regard for the environment.
Throughout, the printing and binding have been planned to ensure a sturdy, attractive
publication which should give years of enjoyment. If your copy fails to meet our
high standards, please inform us and we will gladly replace it.

www.musicsales.com

CD Track Listing

Full performance versions...

1. Lotty's Shadow Dance
2. Always Ask Me
3. The Irish Jig (with claps and knee slaps)
4. I Went To The Beach
5. Teddy's Exercise Poem
6. Loch Scridan
7. Water Is Heavy And Noisy!
8. Little Lamb
9. Three Brothers
10. Fred
11. The Choo-Choo Train

Backing tracks only (without vocals)...

12. Always Ask Me
13. The Irish Jig (without claps and knee slaps)
14. I Went To The Beach
15. Loch Scridan
16. Little Lamb
17. Three Brothers
18. Fred
19. The Choo-Choo Train

All tracks © Copyright Chester Music

To remove your CD from the plastic sleeve,
Lift the small lip on the side to break the perforated flap.
Replace the disc after use for convenient storage.